Sharks

Nurse Shark

by Deborah Nuzzolo

Consulting Editor: Gail Saunders-Smith, PhD

Consultant: Jody Rake, member
Southwest Marine/Aquatic Educators' Association

Capstone press®

Mankato, Minnesota

Pebble Plus is published by Capstone Press,
151 Good Counsel Drive, P.O. Box 669, Mankato, Minnesota 56002.
www.capstonepress.com

1 2 3 4 5 6 14 13 12 11 10 09

Library of Congress Cataloging-in-Publication Data
Nuzzolo, Deborah.
    Nurse shark / by Deborah Nuzzolo.
    p. cm. — (Pebble plus. Sharks)
    Includes bibliographical references and index.
    ISBN-13: 978-1-4296-2261-5 (hardcover)
    ISBN-10: 1-4296-2261-X (hardcover)
    1. Nurse shark — Juvenile literature. I. Title. II. Series.
QL638.95.G55N89 2009
597.3 — dc22   2008022011

Summary: Simple text and photos describe nurse sharks, where they live, and what they do.

Editorial Credits
Jenny Marks, editor; Ted Williams, set designer; Kim Brown, book designer; Jo Miller, photo researcher

Photo Credits
Alamy/Arco Images GmbH/Hinze K, 5
Corbis/Reuters/David Loh, 9; Stephen Frink, 21
Peter Arnold/Jonathon Bird, 7, 11
Photo Researchers, Inc/Louise Preston, 1
Seapics/Jason Pickering, 15
Seapics.com, 17, 19; D. R. Schrichte, cover
Tom Stack & Associates, Inc./Tom Stack, 13

Note to Parents and Teachers

The Sharks set supports national science standards related to the characteristics and behavior of animals. This book describes and illustrates nurse sharks. The images support early readers in understanding the text. The repetition of words and phrases helps early readers learn new words. This book also introduces early readers to subject-specific vocabulary words, which are defined in the Glossary section. Early readers may need assistance to read some words and to use the Table of Contents, Glossary, Read More, Internet Sites, and Index sections of the book.

Table of Contents

Night Sharks

Nurse sharks

are night animals.

They hunt all night

and rest all day.

Nurse sharks live
in warm, shallow water.

They lie on the sea bottom.

Sometimes they pile
on top of each other.

Nurse Shark Pups

Pups are born

in sea grass beds

or coral reefs.

About 20 to 30 pups

are born at a time.

9

What They Look Like

Nurse sharks have yellow-brown bodies and fins.

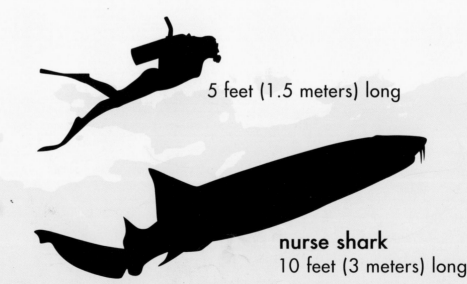

5 feet (1.5 meters) long

nurse shark
10 feet (3 meters) long

Nurse sharks have wide heads.

Barbels hang under their snout.

Like small fingers,

barbels search for food.

Hunting

Hungry nurse sharks
hunt for fish, crabs,
and animals that hide
in the sand.

Nurse sharks have

many small, strong teeth.

Their teeth crush

the hard shells

of clams and lobsters.

To eat, a nurse shark

quickly sucks food

into its mouth.

It can even suck

a snail from its shell.

Small sea animals

should fear nurse sharks.

But these shy sharks

are only dangerous to people

if they're bothered.

Glossary

barbel — a whiskerlike feeler on the head of some fish

coral reef — a type of land made up of a hardened group of corals; corals are small, colorful sea creatures.

dangerous — not safe

pup — a young shark

sea grass — a type of plant that grows in the sea

shallow — not deep

snout — the front part of an animal's head that sticks out

Read More

Lindeen, Carol K. *Sharks.* Under the Sea. Mankato, Minn.: Capstone Press, 2005.

Simon, Seymour. *Sharks!* New York: Collins, 2006.

Thomson, Sarah L. *Amazing Sharks!* An I Can Read Book. New York: HarperCollins, 2005.

Internet Sites

FactHound offers a safe, fun way to find educator-approved Internet sites related to this book.

Here's what to do:

1. Visit *www.facthound.com*

2. Choose your grade level.

3. Begin your seach.

This book's ID number is 9781429622615.

FactHound will fetch the best sites for you!

Index

Word Count: 148
Grade: 1
Early-Intervention Level: 18